strange and beautiful

An *Artists Lifeline* Publication

strange and beautiful

Poems Copyright © 2006-2010 by Lindsey Watson

Published by
Artists Lifeline, LLC
Honolulu, Hawai`i, USA

Website: http://www.artistslifeline.com

Front Cover Photo: "Frozen" by Lindsey Watson © 2006
Back Cover Photo © 2007 by Allen J. Miller

FIRST EDITION

ISBN 978-0-9831492-0-0

An *Artists Lifeline* Publication

strange and beautiful

strange and beautiful

strange and beautiful

DEDICATION

These poems are about the people who

spin you
twist you
bleed you
fill you
love you
hate you

the people you can't let go

Lindsey Watson
November, 2010

strange and beautiful

No Regrets, No Remorse

Broken dreams seldom fix themselves
all hopes and good intentions
crumble under the weight of reality
whispers and wind-blown secrets
block doorways that long to be closed
or opened, either way they let in a draft
fantasies behind black curtains
soaked with rain; the tears of the sky
abstract conversations
broken through morse code
reveal the meaning of life
no regrets
no remorse
live to love
even if it ends in
broken dreams and good intentions

Mirror Images

Two people
One face
Two souls
Two minds

Mirror images

I am a separate person!
I am my own!

Identical eyes
Matching smiles

Can you hear our cries?
They are opposite

Can you see our dreams?
They are different

Must we always be seen
as

Mirror images
One face
Matching smiles

Two souls

Please let us be separate people

You get angry

You get angry
that's what death does
A light
A warmth on my face
The breeze through my hair
I smell the trees

You get angry
that's what death does
A heartbeat
A silent scream
Sinking
A coldness creeps in
Shadows dance in your eyes

You get angry
that's what death does
Not a death of the flesh
A death of the heart
The funeral of love
The welcoming of silence

Where you used to whisper...
I love you

Nightmares and Daydreams

I don't sleep
anymore

My dreams
nightmares

My daydreams
worse

No dream
can give me
you

No fantasy
can grant me
love

Nightmares
awaken me
To breathe,
blink
see
Daymares

Cello

When I die
let me be
reborn into
a tree

The strong
and beautiful
kind

Let me be made
into a cello

and place me
in loving hands

So that in love
I may sing
out beautiful
melodies

And that in pain
my strings
may cry tears
in an eerie
haunting
tune

After Him

After him
anything was possible

He showed me how
to love again
To find beauty in everything
around me

He broke my heart
and gave me pain
a different kind of
inspiration

I wouldn't change it
I would take nothing back

I loved
I laughed
I broke
I cried

but through it all —
I *lived*

After him,
anything was possible

They Say I Am A Writer

They say I am a writer

I write;
not really
I follow

They look at my work
"How beautiful
How lovely"

But they do not understand

The breaks
in the line
the emotion
hanging
in every word

They say I am a writer

I say I am a
lover of words
and writing is my way
of loving
caring
caressing
my love for words

Attic Of Imagination

I sit here in the
    attic of my imagination
talking to the faeries and gnomes
    about love

Asking the dragons and knights
    how to be strong
Questioning the wizards and elves
    on the laws of life

We dance and sing
    They show me the brilliant colors
of their worlds

They help inspire my imagination
    and watch over my dreams
Sometimes they speak through me
    in beautiful words
        that I always forget
            to write down

Everyone needs an attic
    like this

It helps to make reality
    a little more bearable

Always There...
Always You

I have bathed in the light of love
lived in its nighttime glow
I'm in a rowboat going backwards
I dial a number I don't know
to hear the voice I cannot forget
I always wish it was real
to hear you speak my name
could destroy my fragile fortress
crafted from the tears of sleepless nights
they shine like diamonds
in the right light
still I crave
that which could kill me
as I live each tomorrow in memories
each night I follow you
into the darkness
where I can still imagine we are in love

I opened myself

I opened myself
vulnerable
exposed

You wrapped me in —
your love
your heart

Our souls connected
if only briefly
then you were
gone

Flying free
over hilltops
and mountain ranges

The colors
of you
Painting the most
beautiful
sunsets

I am
grateful
to know
that for a moment
in time
I was loved by you

I opened myself
vulnerable
exposed

I was
granted
love

A perfect memory
of an imperfect person

I will carry
the imprint of you
with me
      Always

Don't Interrupt Me

Don't interrupt me

There is something I must say

I love you

Oh, that felt good

I love you
I always will

I'm sorry for whatever I did
To drive you away

Forgive my clumsy thoughts
Forgive my insecurities
Forgive my need for you
Forgive my openness

Don't interrupt me

There is one more thing I need to say

I will always love you

You will burn bright in my memory
You will help me through the darkness

I will miss you

I wish you would stay

I will not say goodbye
    I don't mean it
I won't lie

I will just say

I love you

Alone

No Mirrors

There are no mirrors here

I don't want to see me
    without you

My empty eyes
My forced smile

A shattered shell of me

I took them all down
    and threw them away

No ghosts in the mirrors
    to haunt me

Only in my heart

Where there once was love
    now there is pain
Where there was once beauty
    now scarred
Where there once was peace
    now confusion

There are no mirrors here

I need no reminders
    that you're gone

I can feel the wind blow
    through the empty space
        that was once you

Do you think of me?

Do you see me anymore
   when you close your eyes?

Can you sit in silence and hear
   my heart whisper your name?

When you smile and laugh
   do you think of me?

You used to count the minutes
   til you could come home to me

And we'd talk
   how we'd talk
hours passed like minutes
   and then it was time
to return to our lives

Then one night
   you never came home

My heart breaks to
   think we are standing in the dark
right before each other
   but neither knowing how
to say the first word

I still come home at night
    and wait for you
I'd wait for you always
    it's all I can do

Do you still see me anymore
    when you close your eyes?

Remember To Breathe

I wanted you to know
   I still think about you

There are times during my day
   when time momentarily
      stops

And in these brief pauses
   these gaps in reality
     I think of you

Maybe a memory
   of a shared laugh
or a colorful conversation

I loved those

Maybe just a thought
   wondering how you are
if you're happy

Do you ever think of me?

Maybe a wish for you
   to find your happiness
to always be the beautiful
   person that you are

I wish you love

Then it's over
   and life resumes

But after each pause
   each gap spent
      thinking of you

I have to
      Remember to breathe

Fears

I have many fears

Some dark and scary
     others
childish but real

Fears that I have
     conquered
Fears that linger in
     the edge of my vision

I bite my lip
     and turn the other way
yet the feeling of that fear lurking,
     is burning a hole through me

My greatest fear?

I would think that
     was obvious

It has completely
     taken me
turning my world into
     a breathing nightmare

Living without you

When the Sun Sets

The days are long
    but I get by

They aren't as long
    as the nights

Dreaming is the hardest part

Most would say breathing
    but no
I can breathe just fine
    how odd

But when the sun sets
    the stars come out
to laugh at me
    as I wait for you

I finally go to bed
    and walk into my dreams
        So vivid
        So real
         So painful

Breathing doesn't bother me
but dreaming always
    makes me cry

Twilight Lovers

Soaring through the darkness
The stars cry our names
as we begin our game
of hide and seek

Behind Jupiter
around Saturn's rings
Pluto's too cold
So why would you hide there

Come, let's go to Venus
where we always had
our picnics
Or over to Mars
where we'd dance
and talk for hours

I know
Let's go back to Earth

Let's return
and find each other
all over again

Maybe this time
we'll get it right
and in that first moment
before that first touch

We'll see the stars again
and hear laughter
drifting slowly down
from the moon

The wind will surround you
and you will hear
I love you

We will look at one another
and decide
Will things be the same
this time?

Or will we finally give in
to the love
that even the stars
weep for

A Haven

I come here to be
    with myself
To toss rocks into
    the waters
While I think about
    trying to let you go

I climb the rocks
    jagged paths
til I am standing
    on the edge
looking out across
    the water

I can look down
    and see the
undulating, broken images
    of what lies beneath
the surface
    It reminds me
of me
Transparent, but not
    showing my actual self

The rocks comfort me
    the sounds of the waves
sing me a beautiful song

I came here to forget you
    but found myself instead
Staring back at me
    from under my own
Reflection in the water

Still Waters

The water goes on
    for miles and miles
Giving a home and a
    beautiful site to many

You leave the land
    so trusting
to make this journey
    across the waters

Do you leave behind your fears?
Or do you carry them with you?

It's so quiet and peaceful
    the sky and the sea
joining somewhere that
    no man can reach

Out there, on the water
    there is nothing to hide you
from yourself

Then you see it
        off in the distance
land rising up out of
        the horizon
separating the water
        from the sky

For a time
        everything was real
beautiful
        natural

Now it's time to return
        to man-made places
and let the beautiful ones
        remain in your memory

Loves Excessive Force

Our love was like
   the ocean

Calm and serene
   Beautiful and Inviting
Powerful and dangerous

We surrounded ourselves
   in our love
Our passion for life
   and one another
Painted rainbows
   in every inch of the sky

The stars rained down
   lighting up the night
Throwing off shadows
   and revealing
our intertwined souls

I guess when I woke up
   and found myself
Standing
   alone
      on the shore
With the stars once more
Shining
   stationary
      in the velvet sky
And our rainbows
Gone
   vanished
      into the storm clouds
Gathering over the sea
   to release their
first wave
   of mourning

I should have known

A love like ours
   has to end
with excessive force

And what could be
   more forceful
than to disappear
   into the shadows
that our love
   once mocked

Nowhere

You're walking away
    I feel the world

Tilting

How is it that I can
    just let you leave?

My feet are stuck,
    nailed to the ground
with confusion

You said you'd never leave
    Stupid me
I believed you

I tried to scream
    no words came out
I cried and cried
    trying to get your attention

But you just left
    So cold
    So hollow
    So unlike the man
I fell in love with

I guess
    I always feared
it would end
    But I never dreamed
it would end
    So impersonal
like strangers parting
    from a crowded train
that I forgot to get off of

Now I'm lost
    somewhere
but really
    Anywhere is nowhere
if you're no longer
    here

The Real Question

Tell me what to do
    with your memories

I keep going through
    these boxes labeled
"Him"

I keep walking through
    the gallery
of my imagination
    — your eyes
always bring me to
    tears

I am slowly
    losing touch
with reality

But then again
    what do you care?

That's just it though!

I know you did

That could not have been
     a lie

I guess the real question
     I am trying to ask is

Why did you stop?

A Love's Devotion

She gets up
    every morning
drinks her coffee
    black
as she picks out her clothes

Fixes her hair
    make-up just right
and makes the drive
    across town
up the elevator
    room 519

Everyone smiles
    nods
shakes their heads
    as she walks past
but on she walks
    head high

She opens the door
    T.V. voices
echoing off the walls
    she tells them to always
turn it on
    for the games shows
he likes

Putting down
   her bag
she leans over
   his bed
and whispers
   Good Morning
       My love

No warm grettings
   answered her back
only slow breathing as she
   places a light kiss
on his forehead
   and squeezes
his limp hand

Still calloused
   after all this time
Light tobacco stains
   still linger on his
fingertips

She brushes
   his hair
and changes
   his clothes
as he sleeps

She tells him
    of the children
and how her roses
    are blooming early

She moves
    his legs
back and forth
    up and down
as she sings
    him a song from
their wedding

She clips
    his nails
and puts
    lotion
on his hands
    as she sits
silently
    and cries

She collects
    her things
and leans over
    and says

Hurry home
   to me love
So we can talk
   all about
the places
   you have been
and the sights you
   have seen
I love you
   my darling
I'll see you tomorrow

She holds her head up
   and smiles
to the staff
   they admire her
but think her
   foolish

For years he has been
   sleeping
and everyday
   she comes to him
to take care of him
   in a way that they can't
she cares for his soul
   not only his body

This is her
  love
This is her
  devotion

No matter
  what they say
She believes
  he will come back to her

It's only a matter
  of time
And without him
  time
is all she has

I miss my friend

I love you
yes, that's true

I miss you
more than I can ever say

You know what I miss the most

The talks
I loved talking to you

For hours and hours

We never once said
So what do you want to talk about

So naturally
we would fall into our conversations
and oh, how it hurt
to say goodnight

Once,
not so long ago
we were best friends

I miss my friend
Do you miss me?

Although I am Two

Although I am two
    I feel
    I hurt
    I laugh

I speak to you
    but you just smile
and go on your way

I scream and cry
    'cause I don't know
any other way to get you
    to see me

Everything is new to me
    colors
        lights
            words
I feel
    but I don't know what

I need for you
    to teach me
all about this life

Although I am two
   I am real

Won't you help me be
     as great as you
wanted to be

Only a Kiss

There it goes
    that long lingering
look

The one that
    speaks a thousand words
at volumes
    that sound can't match

My stomach
    flips
knees
    go weak
I hold
    my breath
I wonder
    can you hear
my heart beating too?

Your hand
    brushes mine
Did you mean
    to do that?
You smile
    I smile
we both
    shift in our seats

Palms
   sweating
Mouth
   dry
Thoughts
   racing
Your hand
   my face
Time stops
   your lips
brush mine
   heart
      beating
        so hard
          or
            is that
              yours
we melt
   together
then slowly
   pull apart

Your eyes
   my soul
we both
   shift
nervously

It was only
   a kiss

Lady Winter

Lady winter
    finally
        caught up
            with me

She has laid down
    a blanket
        of her
            white tears
masking the world
    in her
        chillingly
            cold beauty

Snow faeries laugh
    and dance
        on the drifts
        at us
and how we call winter
    beautiful

This is
    Lady winter's
        way
of remembering
    a love
        lost
            forgotten
                abandoned

Each snow flake is
    one more tear
        that she
            sheds
                in her
yearly moments of
    weakness

Thinking about

I wake in the mornings
and go about my day

Thinking about
    not thinking
        about you

I laugh with friends
I smile to strangers

And think about
    not thinking
        about you

I pretend I'm happy
Sometimes
    I don't pretend to be

Thinking about
   not thinking
      about you

But at the end of the day

I turn down the bed

Blow out the lights

And think about
   not thinking
      about you

Only For You

You bring a peace to my soul
like standing in the sun
during a light rain
When you speak
all my troubles melt away
in the maple flavored sound
of your voice
There's magic in your touch
every inch of my
skin aching to be
all over you
beside you
around you

Forever is in your eyes
taking me by the hand
to the green hills
of Montana
the deep blues of the ocean
the earth tones of the desert

I want to tell you
how much I love you
but it all sounds like
Hi to me
and *me too* holds more
emotion than two words should
but only
for you

Stalling

Move slowly
recheck your bag
your pockets
forget where you put
your keys
Stall
I'm stalling too
Stand still
don't breathe or blink
maybe if we pretend that
time has stopped
the sun won't rise
and you won't have to leave
I hear the birds
it smells like morning
Hold me love!
it's almost time
fingertips and skin
hands and eyes
burning memories that
will carry us til
we are together again

I can't open the door
kiss me again
don't let go
frantic hands trying to
make a minute last forever;
a look
a kiss
I love you
then I am on my doorstep
and your tail lights are
turning around the corner
I'm crying now
and the sun rises

Skin

Can one fully explain
the magic of
skin on skin?

the loudest conversations
between held hands
or the sweet nothings
whispered with
the brush of fingertips
across the face
all the love conveyed
as cheek to cheek
you hold one another
falling asleep feeling
your lover's heartbeat
against your bare back
all the joy in eskimo kisses
and the passion as two sets
of lips meet and find
they fit together as if
crafted purposely
one for the other

or all the pain from
a goodbye embrace
the kind that slides away
til only the tips of the fingers
are holding on
trying hard to let go
but stay at the same time
Sometimes there are
no words that need
to be spoken
but felt
skin to skin

One Night

I like to remember you
over coffee and curls of smoke
your hands
your eyes
your lips
vibrant memories of
emotions that swelled
and burst in one night

oh, but in the night
I was yours completely
and you were mine
lips full of passion
touches shaking an already
fragile body
colors so loud that one sigh
shattered them into silence

I left you in the morning
with a smile and a kiss
on your sleeping face
I wanted to know you
instead I walked out the door
into the real world
leaving you in a room
that wasn't real
yet it felt real
for one night

Nowhere Near the Neighborhood

I was
   nowhere near the neighborhood
but I wanted
   to tell you

You're heartless
   but I love you

You're cold
   and cruel
but my heart beats
   only for you

You're a coward
   yet ruthless
but I can't get you
   out of my head

You're dark
   and deadly
but you've never been
   more beautiful
      to me

Red Lace

Red lace
    soft against my skin
I felt so vulnerable and stupid
    but you made
all that disappear
    and I felt
        beautiful
under your gaze

You said that I
    took your breath away
You always knew
    the perfect words
the ones that made me feel
    amazing

Things change
Time passed
    and now
the red lace feels like
    razors against my skin

What was once so
    delicate and beautiful
turned into something
    tainted and ugly

Your spin was nice
    you are a master
at your game

Not everyone can make
    me feel

so beautifully dirty

I Keep You

There is no rushing river
or thundering waterfall
that can speak louder
than a sigh from your lips

as the water accepts
and cradles me
I know your hands are softer
than this aquatic kiss

The gentle butterfly
knowing only tenderness
in their brief lifetime
cannot know the freedom
I feel in your arms

There's no forgotten garden
tucked away in the protective forest
surrounded by serenity and stillness
that can capture the purest feelings
passed through me
a peace when you touch my hair

I keep you quietly in my heart

Comfortable Silence

I dreamt of you last night

    Nothing spectacular
    Nothing cruel or unkind
       It was just you

We stood for awhile
    simply staring at one another
No shared kisses
    no longing embraces

We just sat together
    listening to the wind
and watching the stars

    Comforted in our silence

I looked at you
    "ya know"
You smiled softly at me
    "yeah, I know"

The Hourglass

The hourglass drops
the last few grains of sand
    a light goes out
    a light goes on
    a life takes a final breath
    a life cries for the first time
they are one
the hourglass turns and starts
again
across the world
a heart is tuned to an echoed cry
of a lost lover

time goes by
the sands fall
two hearts are joined
    (are torn apart)
the sands keep falling

two hands
wrinkled but firm
holding tight
a moment together
waited on an entire lifetime
or two or three
a whisper
   I'll find you
a nod
the hourglass drops
the last few grains of sand
a final breath
a solitary tear
a light goes out

a baby cries
and an old man
miles and miles away
smiles
somewhere deep
his heart hears her cry
and soon he will pass this life
and begin anew
he will find her again

I'll find you

each life one step closer
to stopping the hourglass
that turns and turns
and turns

Behind Windows

helplessness consumes me.
I watch through the windows
that used to be my eyes
my body has now become
my prison. I can't get out
can't lift my hands or
move my feet. I can't speak
or breathe. Yet through
these windows I can see
(although it rains a lot).

Sometimes while standing
at these windows I watch
silently as you fall apart
in front of me. Your fear
and confusion run through
your small body and I am helpless
as I watch you attack yourself
then retreat and I see
another set of windows
and a small scared child
with hands upon the glass
looking out at the world
that drives her in. I stand
pounding weightless fists
on shatterproof glass
So that I can try and save
my little girl from a life
behind windows

Summer of '93

I lost myself
in the summer of '93
with confusion and
good intentions and
the desire to fit it
funny how a landslide
can build from
admiration and
wanting something so fleeting as
being cool
no one warned me
that it doesn't pay out in life
my brain got foggy and
my good intentions misplaced
somewhere inside
insecurity and the need to be loved
too bad my proverbial heart
mixed sex up with genuine feelings
but somehow it didn't matter
it was all slipping away
and soon I was making friends
physically

sadly it was then I realized
I achieved my goal
the one that started
behind an old broke down truck
that summer
I was cool
I was the girl everyone knew and
most called friend
a word as commonly used as love
and demeaned til it barely mattered
I was pretty
I was clean
I was healthy
I was fun
I was easy
I was cold
sex with no strings
and no complications the next day
I was the girl who didn't care
how could anyone feel something for someone
so cold

I never found the girl
who laid down behind that truck
but instead joined the stars that watched
her good intention-filled demise
but I miss her
and all she could have been
but at least she died still believing
in a dream that would never happen
starting on her back
behind that truck
in the middle of the night
during the summer of '93

Let Me

I wanted to tell you
that this will be okay
I will hold you through the night
and chase the nightmares away

There's no need for
brave faces and stubborn pride
I can taste the pain in your tears
mixed with salt and longing

Let me do this
I want to help you...fly
there are places we need to go
and lives we need to live

I walk the shores with you
in my dreams and in them you are
smiling and free
I love to see you happy

So cry now love
I am not leaving you here
I will help you remember
pure tears cleanse the soul

and that love
is all that you deserve

Unintentional Complications

you kissed·my head last night
how can this be the memory I want to keep
There is nothing about this relationship
(to even call it that seems ridiculous)
that warrants such an intimate gesture
We serve a purpose in each other's lives
We substitute and stimulate
but that's it
(isn't it)
There was never any intention for feelings
no room, no need, we each have that
Our arrangement
(almost like a contract, planned to the T)
was for gratification and desire only
a means to walk on the wild side
and give in to carnal desires
(the pull was a bit too strong though, wasn't it)
but emotions were to be checked at the door
like a coat too heavy to wear at dinner
(the signal was the turning of the lock in the door)
So when I was down, tired and beaten
you showed me a side that scares me
taking me in your arms was nothing new
(I know these arms, my lips have memorized them)

you made no move
a hug
something that was unnatural for us
(there's another term that's odd, but growing)
you held me close then
BAM!
everything changed
We had terms!
an agreement
Damn it! we had rules!
no intimacy
I don't need it
nor do I want it
I have love in my life
a heart that has been broken
and superglued back together so many times
(Van Gogh would love the results)
but yet, I have tucked this memory in my heart
this tender kiss
and it festers and threatens to infect me
with emotions that are dangerous to both of us
(please don't do this)
it was great
we were having fun

Now all I can feel is that kiss
all I can see are your eyes
all I can smell is your skin
all I can hear is your voice
telling me that this will all be okay
but I know it wont
I can feel it in my stomach
a burning in my soul
building like a pop bottle about to explode
I am falling for you
and nothing is going to be okay

This Pen Drips Poison

This pen drips poison
in growing puddles
that infest and consume
those who read

A slow consumption as it hits the blood
pumping confusion and rage towards
the heart, who upon ingestion
swells, flares, and dies.
The brain becomes foggy
wasted time turns to days
dwelling on a misery that greets you by name
and kisses your hand at the door

I watch helplessly in charge
and cry at the outcome that
plays on DVD round the clock
in technicolor, flat screen, latest model!
die in style they say

I can't counter the poison
and there will be no vaccine
but a cure that springs forth
as I lay down this pen
and walk away
no words, no hopes, no regrets, no more

Maps

The tulips are blooming
red and yellow dots
on this map that
brings me directions
to you in the fragrance
of raspberries
The moon shines down
and the stars come out
little dots flashing me
directions to you
if I look close enough
I can see your face
mirrored in these stars
and I know you are looking
at them too
The Spring breeze brings
your laughter
from the west
the windmills spinning
helping the breeze bring me
directions to you
Everything around me
has become a way to remind me
that all maps lead to you.

Flirting

Teasing touches
quiet laughter
eyes that meet
hold
then look away
a quickened pulse
brought on by accidental
brushes of the arm
the air is thick
hot
(and all I want to do is kiss you)
smiles
flirting becomes the game
never alone
(I don't trust myself with you)
but in daydreams
things go very differently
exploring fingertips
tracing nervous skin
(I'm holding my breath)
these things never happen
not fully
leaving me with only
teasing touches

A Dream's Embrace

I want you to photograph me
you tell me you can't
"I only play with pictures
I cannot do you justice"
but I want you to photograph me

I tell you I am no model
"but when you look at me
I feel beautiful"
you tell me you can't
but I'm not asking anymore

a camera lays inside your hand
I'm waist deep in the river
my long hair grazing the surface
a surface that with the help of the moon
causes my skin to glow and I feel like a night angel

I hear you whisper, to yourself, to me,
to the quiet waters around us
"I am no photographer"
but as I turn my head to look at you
I hear it,
Click
and I am smiling
I knew you couldn't resist

water at my shoulders
I feel like a star
shining brightly on a summer's night
maybe I can be the one lovers wish on
just for this moment
I submerge myself in the river
I can feel your surprise turn to fear
and then you hear me
somewhere deep inside yourself
"Wake up, wake up and come and find me"
your protest need not be verbal but they are anyways
I can feel you desperately trying to stay asleep
"but how will I find you?"
you're still floating to reality
there is no way to win this fight
you will wake up, just like every night before
"Come to me, you know where I am,
you have always known."
The light from the window breaks through heavy
eyelids
 as you realize, the dream is over
 the haze is fading and the mist is rolling back and I
hear
"I will find you"
I wake up, miles and miles from that shining river
and his camera
not sure who is dreaming here
me, or him

Too Late

pokes

you'd miss me, wouldn't you?

smiles

it'd suck if you left

tilted head

so...you'd miss me?

looks down

yeah, it'd suck

shrugs

you'd miss me
for carnal reasons

jerks head

what!? no

*hand under chin
thumb running over lips*

I'd miss you
not your body
or the fun things we do
but you

smiles

I knew you'd miss me

leaning closer

yeah, I'd miss you

lips touching, barely

I thought we weren't
gonna let this get
messy and complicated?

*eyes shining
a soft smile*

too late

Creating

The moon spills through
the open window
summoning the sounds of
crickets to sing along
with the piano
echoing softly from the speakers

I was molding him to my touch
soft skin under my hands
he would be my greatest creation
a light trace of the jawbone
punctuating each stroke with a kiss
my lips counting out his ribs
closed protectively around a heart
the world was not ready for

My hands on his stomach
drawing pictures with each
rise and fall of his chest
crawling up to his face
where his eyes hold emotions
that could light the planet afire

An exhausted ballet of lovers
connecting
creating
succumbing
to all the things that need to be felt
never spoken

The moon spills through
the open window
he will be my greatest creation

He asks
" How do you do it?"

I say
" I breathe..."

Again

Again sounds nice
to fall into old patterns
of laughter and nicknames
"I love you's" and "Forevers"

How I longed, cried, and prayed
for the word "Again" til I blocked
all sound and heard only that.
In a time when I still believed
in faerie tales

Instead of "Again" to revive me
I had to find myself, myself
who knew I would be so elusive
found under a rock
in the river

Emerging deep waters
I heard silence
instead of the ever present
record on repeat
that howled "Again"

Again sounds nice
but I can't hear you anymore
and I can't bring myself
to go deaf, again

The birds sing to me

Time heals everything

The Smell Of Salt

The smell of salt pulls me back
how I long to look across waves
into forever
the prospect of losing myself
to the sea, intrigues me

Fly with me across the blue
let the whales scream our names
and catch rides on hurricanes

Swim with me
my sister is a mermaid
and we'll use sharks as our taxis
I know a cave we can live in
but you must leave your bubble
on dry land

We'll go to school with the fish
and learn how to move with the water
and let the current carry us to
new places around the world
I have always wanted to travel

Sink with me into the deep
where the only boundaries are dry
and life moves in time with the moon
pulling at the water
water mixed with blood that
pumps through my veins
calling me home

It's always the smell of salt
that pulls me back

Write Her

Touch the pen to paper
soft as a lover's kiss
burning with all the passion
of the forbidden

Look not to the end
let it play itself out
taking you along for the ride

Succumb to the intensity
of all you are feeling
words exploding on the page
as images of her hair flowing
down a tender back fill your mind

Forget the mistakes of former lovers
they were but preparation for a heart
that engulfs your soul
freeing you from yourself

Open the door and embrace the love
that has haunted your dreams
taste her lips the sweet fruit of desire
feel the soft skin tremble under your touch

Life can be a dream
or dreams can be your life
either way she will haunt them both
every time you let your heart go
and let your pen touch the paper

Couch Cushions

My couch stares at me
whispering secrets that ignite
it smiles and laughs
taunting me with memories of heat

I try to ignore them
in chores beyond my living room
visitors come
they sit and laugh
making small talk
that is never small
I smile and nod
not seeing busybodies perched
on fading fabric
but lovers dancing
worshipping each other
in the moonlight
that sneaks through broken blinds

I run my fingers over the seams
funny how they still feel warm
to my touch
and I smell you, me, passion and need
covered up by fabric softeners

My couch teases me with thoughts of us
and I think that these cushions
miss you as much as I do

Talking To The Moon

I want to call you
heartless
but I can't convince myself of that
it would be easier if you were
then I wouldn't be spending
countless nights talking to the moon
trying to figure out how
a soul mate leaves
how sad that the lonely moon
doesn't even know that answer
to figure that out
you would have to travel
past beautiful curls
and eyes that never end
to the deepest parts of
a dreamer's soul
past the coffin which holds his heart
and past the hill
where daydreams were nightdreams
shared by two
settled by one
now harbouring the ghost of
the forgotten
if you do this, if you turn the lock
and peek inside
keep the answers to yourself
I'll keep talking to the moon

waiting for my dreamer
to come and sit beside me and tell me
of his heart's desire
to tell me I am one of them
and if he never comes
then I will wait
what's one more lifetime
spent talking to the moon
of two hearts molded together
through time and space

Borrowed Looking Glass

There is this feeling of complete peace
that passes the levels of this world
and take root in the foundation of imagination
when we are together
(a fitting of souls)
Yet there is no hell that can match
the hours, days, months of silence
we put each other (ourselves) through
I wish for a looking glass
(I think I'll borrow Alice's)
that, once entered,
delivers me to you on our hill
(the capital of our combined fantasies)
surrounded by fateful (faithful) stars
I wonder why we are letting them win
we've hurt each other
a failed attempt to spare our split souls
the pain that we are causing ourselves
(but in the end it just hurts)
no worries, no survivors
only lovers who still try and send messages
in the wind

I've loved you
lost you
let you go
yet you never leave
(Alice tells me you still love me
but the rabbit is playing hide and seek
with our hearts instead of the Queen)
I have forgotten you!
or I meant to
but when I close my eyes
and meet you at the end of waking thoughts
I say I love you
to the man I meant to make a stranger
but remains my lost lover
and lives right inside my borrowed looking glass

Strange World

Lost in this strange world
filled with the silent pleas for help
and rain that taste of tears
Nothing filling up the emptiness around me
suffocating
words fall in the language that has no sound
running is fruitless
watching the ground move faster
than my legs won't move
Strangers offer no assistance
sympathetic eyes peek out over
hand-stitched mouths
tears form but never fall
only stay to provide a place of refuge
for the aquatic life which are my dreams
Fear is not found in the conformity to silence
and obedience
but in the ones who cut
the threads from their lips
to try and speak of the beauty in the weeping willows
I may never wake from this hell like dream
but I will not give up
I will find a way to cut the strings
and speak of pain and beauty
and let my tears once more fall from my eyes
instead of the clouds

Unseen Beauty

Such a shame
your beauty falls on
unworthy eyes
the flash of your heart
is wasted
the soul fighting a love
that will not be silent
all reflected under
long eyelashes
but they don't see
many cry out
in hollow fashion
"I love him, I want to love him!"
I listen and watch
these empty declarations of love
hurt you more than they entice your smile
yet, you still love to smile
I think to myself
I don't know how to stop loving you

Walking in your Eyes

sleepless nights spent
walking in your eyes
running my fingertips in the
crystal blue waters of your soul
I long to open myself
to share you underneath the moon
and wake each morning
looking into the most beautiful eyes
ever gifted to mortal beings
private smiles shared across a crowded room
stolen moments to succumb to the
deepest kiss that merges soul to soul
not simply mouth to mouth
A falling into love, life, freedom
running through busy hours that creep by
all bringing me back to you
til I am forced once again to spend
sleepless nights
walking in your eyes

The Curve of Your Lips

It was the curve of your lips
that stopped me in my tracks
such a lovely mouth fixed
with an accidental pout that
flourished when you smiled
I wanted to run my thumb over
those lips
to lightly hold them between mine
as our breath came in short gasps
to let them dance
your hands in my hair
eyes open
eyes closed
eyes open
you're still there
so oblivious to the
curve of your lips

Reckless Perfection

The flash of a smile
echoes of laughter
weaving in and out
lost in a wave of faces

a little game of cat and mouse
something to entertain the mind
while the flesh burns hotter

The faint smell
of memories past
a light touch
skin on skin
such a rush cannot be found
in drink or drug
the erotic high
of bodies on fire
a quickened pulse
can infect the strongest man

(I feel beautiful and you allow
me to share this beauty with you)

The pressure of the wall
at my back
I can feel your heart beating
bump
bump
bump
hard against my own
in perfect time
hands making paths
on skin alive with desire

drawing out each touch
my tongue dances
denying the victory of your mouth
instead teasing with a brush
jagged breath's
the longer this takes
the more time stolen
is worth every risk that lies behind
one night of reckless perfection

Beautiful Disaster

Such a bittersweet dream
your angels are your demons
running beside your black cloud
each racing to the sunset
one to admire one to destroy
taking you along for the ride
they eat at your soul
yet leave the pain where it is
glowing in your discomfort
laughing yet unsure
as you fight for all that you adore
and that which you despise
but it's all still yours
your heart
your life
your memories
your beauty
Hold on, you are the only one
who can send them to the flame
although you are a disaster
what a beautiful disaster you are

Together

I still meet you in my dreams
where we talk and "I love you"
needs only be said with our eyes
I feel you in the wind
you caress my face
and I feel safe in my own skin
My heart still echos yours
two beats
one sound
I ask not for your return
how do you return what never left?
Words may be lost
hours waste away
separated
I never walked away
rooted to this hill
waiting
then realizing
I never had to look
for you were always here
as I am always there
behind closed eyelids
we dance in dreams
to our silent hearts
we are still
together

Me Too

Tonight
I'm alone with you
only with me
I hold you close
catching smoke with my hands
gazing at eyes that only I can see
a presence so strong
even imaginary it's overwhelming
I tell you my secrets and let you in my thoughts
You tell me of your fears
and how you love when my hair falls in my eyes
because it gives you a reason to touch my face
We spend hours in silence
speaking all we cannot say
as the sun rises and you begin to fade
I whisper
I need you more than I should
you smile and then you're gone
and all I hear is
me too

Come Home

If it's not too much to ask
can the wind blow this way?
The world is off
and the music has lost its sound
while you are off chasing yourself(me)
You're here(never left)
why you needed to leave
are your own thoughts
the snow has melted
the leaves have changed(they live)
the sun has come out
the breeze of summer hints
to the trees
that it's time to come home

www.ingramcontent.com/pod-product-compliance
Lightning Source LLC
Chambersburg PA
CBHW061752020426

42331CB00006B/1445